JUDO

Rennay Craats

Weigl Publishers Inc.

Published by Weigl Publishers Inc.
123 South Broad Street, Box 227
Mankato, MN 56002
USA
Copyright © 2002 Weigl Publishers Inc.
Web site: www.weigl.com

Library of Congress Cataloging-in-Publication
Data available upon request from the publisher.
Fax: (507) 388-2746 for the attention of the
Publishing Records Department.
ISBN: 1-930954-22-0

Printed in the United States of America
1 2 3 4 5 6 7 8 9 05 04 03 02 01

Managing Editor
Kara Turner
Layout and Design
Warren Clark
Terry Paulhus
Copy Editor
Jennifer Nault

Photograph credits
Cover: Lou DiGesare/Real Judo Magazine; Corbis
Images: page 4, 7; Lou DiGesare/Real Judo
Magazine: page 3, 5T, 5B, 6, 8, 10L, 12T, 12B, 13L,
13R, 15T, 15B, 16R, 18L, 18R, 19L, 19R, 20R, 21;
Empics Sports Photography Ltd: page 1, 10R, 11, 14,
17, 23; Eyewire: page 20L; Judo British Columbia:
page 16L, 22

Contents

PAGE 4
What is Judo?

PAGE 6
Getting Ready to Play

PAGE 8
The Playing Field

PAGE 10
The Rules of the Dojo

PAGE 12
Learning the Moves

PAGE 14
Throws and Holds

PAGE 16
Amateur to Pro

PAGE 18
Superstars of the Sport

PAGE 20
Training

PAGE 22
Brain Teasers

PAGE 24
Glossary / Index / Web Sites

What is Judo?

Judo has been played for more than 100 years. A man named Jigoro Kano invented the sport in the early 1880s. Kano had studied **jujitsu**, which is an aggressive martial art. Kano wanted young students to learn Japanese methods of hand-to-hand fighting. He also wanted them to be safe. He created judo as a safe fighting form. Unlike jujitsu, Kano's sport did not allow blows or kicks. He began teaching this style of fighting, called *kano-ryu*. The name was later changed to Kodokan judo. In 1886, the Japanese police department held a jujitsu tournament. Kano's students entered and won thirteen of the fifteen matches. After this success, judo was declared an official martial art.

There was a surprise gold medal winner at the 1964 Olympic Games in Tokyo. Anton Geesink from the Netherlands won the open category.

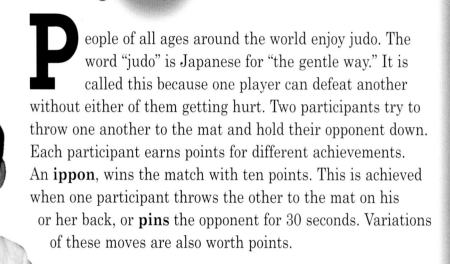

People of all ages around the world enjoy judo. The word "judo" is Japanese for "the gentle way." It is called this because one player can defeat another without either of them getting hurt. Two participants try to throw one another to the mat and hold their opponent down. Each participant earns points for different achievements. An **ippon**, wins the match with ten points. This is achieved when one participant throws the other to the mat on his or her back, or **pins** the opponent for 30 seconds. Variations of these moves are also worth points.

People of all ages can learn judo. Students are expected to train at least twice a week.

CHECK IT OUT

To find out more about judo, surf over to
www.JudoInfo.com

Jimmy Pedro, a U.S. champion, pins an opponent at the 2000 Sydney Olympics.

Getting Ready to Play

A judo school is called a *dojo*. In Japanese, the word "do" means way, road, or path, and the word "jo" means place. So the dojo is "the place of the way." Students training in judo are called *judokas* and the teacher is called *sensei*.

The left side of the jacket crosses over the right side. The sleeves should fall slightly above the wrists so they do not get in the way.

Belts are wrapped around the student's waist twice and tied in a knot. The color shows what level the student is.

During competition, one judoka will sometimes wear a blue outfit. This is so the referee can tell them apart. If both judokas are wearing white, one will wear a different color belt.

Teachers and students wear the same uniform, called a *gi*. A judo gi is made of strong cotton canvas. It has to withstand the throwing and **grappling** that goes on during a match. Judo students are taught to look after their gis. After a class, the gi is folded into a square and tied using the belt. The gi should be washed every time it is used to keep it clean and crisp.

There are nine colors of belt. Students starting out wear white and move up to yellow, orange, green, blue, and brown belts. The higher ranked judoka wear black, red with blocks of white, and then solid red—the highest rank.

The pants of the gi usually fall above the ankle. Judoka do not want to trip or get tangled in their pant legs.

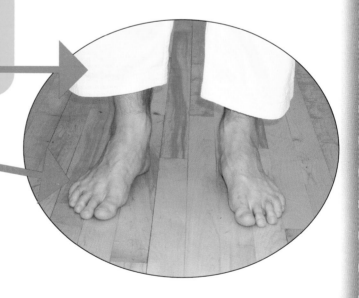

Judoka do not wear anything on their feet. They need to wear shoes only when walking to and from the mat. Judo slippers called *zori* may be worn before and after competing to make sure the mat remains clean.

The Playing Field

The playing area of the dojo is lined with mats. These mats are soft so athletes are not hurt when they are thrown to the ground. Traditionally, straw mats were used in Japanese dojos. Now, mats are rubber or filled with foam. These materials help cushion the fall, but judokas also need to learn how to fall correctly.

Local competitions are an important way for judokas to improve technique and learn new skills. The very best athletes are chosen to compete in international events such as the Olympic Games.

During competition, the entire floor is padded. The playing area is often marked with a red border. The sides of the square playing area need to be between about 26 and 33 feet long. The lines that provide the boundaries of the square are slightly more than 3 feet wide. This is the called the danger area. Players cannot stay in this area for more than 5 seconds at a time.

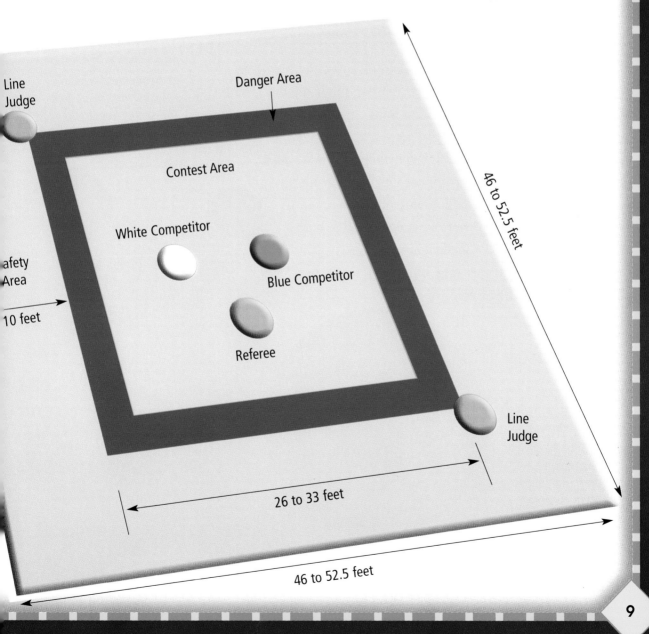

Line Judge

Danger Area

Contest Area

White Competitor

Blue Competitor

Safety Area

10 feet

Referee

46 to 52.5 feet

26 to 33 feet

Line Judge

46 to 52.5 feet

The Rules of the Dojo

A judo match for juniors lasts 4 minutes. Senior judokas play for 5 minutes. Judokas need to stay within the boundaries. If either competitor steps out of bounds for more than 5 seconds, penalty points are given. If both players step outside the lines, the match is stopped. Players return to the middle and the contest continues.

The goal of a judo match is to score an ippon by throwing or pinning an opponent to the mat. The number of points scored depends on how well the judoka does this. If it is done perfectly, an ippon, worth ten points, is awarded. Seven points are given when **tori**, the attacker, throws **uke**, the defender, almost onto his or her back or pins him or her for 25 seconds. Five points are given if tori throws uke onto part of his or her back with less force or pins uke for 20 seconds. Lastly, three points are given if tori pins uke for 10 seconds or trips uke so he or she falls to the mat.

In a competition, both judokas want to be tori. Tori scores points for attacking moves.

If neither judoka scores during a match, the judges and the referee decide who should win.

10

Judokas need to follow the rules. Competitors cannot push their opponents out of the playing area or step out intentionally. They also cannot punch, kick, swear, bite, or use any **banned** throws or holds. A judoka also has to move toward his or her opponent every 20 seconds or be subject to a stalling penalty. *Shido* is a three-point minor penalty for offences such as not advancing on the opponent enough. *Chui* is a five-point penalty given for more serious offences, and *keikoku* is a seven-point penalty given for dangerous offences. A player with two keikoku is **disqualified**.

A judo match is judged by a referee. The referee makes sure the rules are followed and points are scored correctly. Two line judges help the referee. They stand on opposite corners of the mat so they can see any **fouls** along the danger area. If both line judges disagree with the referee, they can overrule him or her.

Points can be scored by pinning uke on his or her back. The hold will not count if the competitors' legs become tangled.

CHECK IT OUT

Find out about the United States Judo Federation at

www.usjf.com

Learning the Moves

One of the most important parts of judo is learning how to fall without being hurt. These moves are called breakfalls. Rather than just hitting the mat and stopping, judokas learn to tuck and roll. They also slap the mat with an open palm or arm to **absorb** some of the force of the fall. Judokas are taught these skills before ever learning to throw or hold an opponent.

Soft practice mats are used when judokas are learning breakfalls.

Often, tori will continue to fight when uke is on the ground, using a ground hold to score extra points.

Throwing is the core of judo. There are three basic throws. Tori can flip uke forward, backward, or to the side. There are different ways to complete these moves. Tori may use various hand and foot positions for the same general throw. To start with, throws are learned in slow motion. Once judokas can throw without thinking about it, they speed up the move.

Judokas need strength and skill. To score points, they also need good balance and coordination.

Side throws are called *ashi waza*. These are often the hardest throws to learn. Each stage of the throw needs to be perfectly timed for it to work. The *de ashi barai* throw uses a one-foot sweep while the *okuri ashi barai* uses a two-foot sweep. Some side throws, such as the *hiza guruma*, require both judokas to spin around. This motion helps tori force uke to the mat.

The speed of today's athletes can make it difficult to judge a match. Sometimes, the referee will consult a video recording before making a final decision.

13

Throws and Holds

Forward and backward throws are called *tachi waza*. Throws are completed by sweeping uke's feet out from under him or her. Competitors can also use their hips to flip opponents onto the mat. They can throw forward while standing on two feet or balanced on one leg. There are several different types of forward throws. *Tai otoshi* and *morote seoi nage* are both forward throws that use different techniques.

There are many different throws in judo. Although some look similar, there are small differences between them, such as the position of the feet.

Backward throws are often used with forward ones. A backward throw puts uke off balance so tori can use a powerful forward throw to score an ippon. Backward throws are usually done while tori balances on one leg. The other leg hooks or sweeps uke's legs out from under him or her. Backward throws often lead to ground fighting. Tori sweeps uke's feet out and then uses ground holds or holds him or her to the mat to score points.

Sayaka Matsumoto (in white) won the silver medal for the U.S. at the 2000 Junior World Championships.

Ground holds are called *ne waza*. These holds are used when a throw has not been completely successful. Points are scored by pinning uke on his or her back. To score for pinning an opponent, tori needs to keep uke's upper body pinned to the mat. Tori also needs to keep his or her own legs away from uke's, for the pin to count. Tori can pin uke in many different positions, including from the side or from the top.

Experienced judokas **spar** with a partner as practice before a competition.

Amateur to Pro

Young children around the world put on their gis and join neighborhood judo clubs. As judokas master the skills, they progress from one belt to the next and from one division to the next. Judokas are bantam until they are about 7 years old. Then they move on to intermediate until they are 11 or 12. Juveniles are usually between 12 and 16. After that, judokas compete as juniors until they are 20.

Men and women compete in one of seven weight categories. Judokas register as heavyweights, half heavyweights, middleweights, half middleweights, lightweights, half lightweights, or extra lightweights. Heavyweight males weigh 220 pounds or more, whereas extra lightweights weigh 132 pounds or less. For women, heavyweights tip the scales at 171.5 pounds or more, and extra lightweights weigh 105.5 pounds or less.

Judokas compete as bantam until they are in the year of their eighth birthday.

In many clubs across the country, children and adults learn judo together.

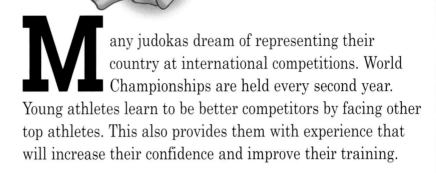

Many judokas dream of representing their country at international competitions. World Championships are held every second year. Young athletes learn to be better competitors by facing other top athletes. This also provides them with experience that will increase their confidence and improve their training.

Serious judokas often strive toward the ultimate international competition—the Olympic Games. Judo has been an Olympic event for men since 1964. The first Olympic judo competition drew seventy-four participants from twenty-seven countries. Now, there are hundreds of judokas from all over the world competing for the medals. Women's judo became an official Olympic sport in 1992. It has become a popular event at the Olympic Games.

These judokas are competing in the heavyweight division at the 2000 Sydney Olympics.

CHECK IT OUT

Read about judo at the Olympics at **www.ipl.org/ref/olympics/judo.html**

Superstars of the Sport

Like most sports, judo has many superstars. They make the sport exciting to watch.

JIMMY PEDRO

DATE OF BIRTH:
October 30, 1970
COUNTRY:
United States

Career Facts:

- Jimmy won a bronze medal at the 1996 Olympic Games in the lightweight division.
- Jimmy was the 1999 World Judo Champion. He did not lose a round during that competition.
- Jimmy was the first American in twelve years and only the third in history to win a world title in judo.
- USA Judo named Jimmy the Male Athlete of the Year in 2000.

RYOKO TAMURA

DATE OF BIRTH:
September 6, 1975
COUNTRY:
Japan

Career Facts:

- Ryoko won the gold medal at the 2000 Olympic Games. She also won silver medals in 1992 and 1996.
- Ryoko competes in the extra lightweight division.
- Ryoko won ten straight National Championships and four straight World Championships.
- The International Judo Federation nominated Ryoko for the "Women and Sport" Trophy for 2001.

SAYAKA MATSUMOTO

DATE OF BIRTH:
December 5, 1982
COUNTRY:
United States

Career Facts:

- Sayaka won gold medals at five National Judo Championships at the junior and senior levels.

- USA Judo named Sayaka the Female Athlete of the Year for 2000.

- Sayaka has won a gold medal, two silver medals, and a bronze medal at international competitions.

- Sayaka won one of these silver medals at the Junior World Championships in Tunisia in October 2000. This earned her the second highest finish ever for an American.

DAVID DOUILLET

DATE OF BIRTH:
February 17, 1969
COUNTRY:
France

Career Facts:

- David won the gold medal at the 2000 Olympic Games. He added this to his gold medal from 1996 and his bronze medal from 1992.

- David was discovered at the age of 8. By age 24 he had won the World Championship.

- "Douillet" means "softie" in French. That name is far from true of the heavyweight champion.

- David was the first Westerner to win both the World Heavyweight and World Open Championships.

CHECK IT OUT

To find out more about Jimmy Pedro, visit

members.nbci.com/jimmypedro/home.html

Training

To be successful, an athlete needs to be healthy. This is true for judokas, too. A healthy, balanced diet of fruit and vegetables, meat, breads, and cereals is important. These foods give people the vitamins, minerals, protein, fiber, and energy they need to keep their bodies strong and working well. Eating regular meals also helps. Athletes need to drink plenty of water while exercising, as well as before and after. The body should always be properly **hydrated**. Sports drinks are also great to have nearby. They help replace the energy and salts that athletes use while working out or competing.

Many judokas are friends. Once a match begins, both competitors are determined to win.

CHECK IT OUT

For the latest news on judo, head to **sports.yahoo.com/oly/judo**

Strong and healthy muscles make judokas ready to hit the mat. Judo is a sport of skill and speed. Judokas need to train to get stronger in these areas. Stretching helps athletes avoid injuries. Judokas can warm up their muscles by running on the spot or by doing jumping jacks. Arm swings, hip rotations, and leg stretches are a part of every judoka's training routine. Each stretch should be held for at least 15 seconds. These exercises get the body ready to do its best during a competition or training session.

Leg stretches are an important part of the warmup before training and competitions. Everyone from beginners to Olympic athletes should stretch before starting any exercise.

Brain Teasers

How much do you know about judo? See if you can answer these questions!

Q What does President Theodore Roosevelt have to do with judo?

A In 1902, President Roosevelt's personal trainer was one of Jigoro Kano's students. The president practiced regularly in a special room in the White House.

Q Why do judokas bow?

A It is a Japanese tradition to bow to each other when meeting or saying goodbye. Judokas bow in the dojo to show respect for their sensei and for their opponents.

Q Judo comes from the Japanese concept of *ju*. What is ju?

A Ju is the practice of meeting violence with non-violence. Students learn to use the force of an opponent against him or her rather than meeting aggression with force of their own.

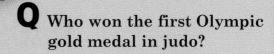

Q Why did Jigoro Kano learn martial arts?

A When growing up, Kano was much smaller than his classmates. He was also often sick. He needed to find a way to defend himself against the bullies at school, so he decided to learn jujitsu.

Q Who won the first Olympic gold medal in judo?

A In 1964, the Olympic Games were held in Tokyo, Japan. Everyone was shocked when Anton Geesink, a Dutch athlete, beat the other competitors, including the Japanese. He won the gold medal in the open category.

Q What is *kata*?

A Kata is a series of rehearsed movements that helps students learn the sport. Each kata has a set sequence of moves.

Glossary

absorb: reduce the effects of

banned: not allowed

disqualified: disallowed from competing as punishment for breaking the rules or for bad behavior

fouls: actions that are against the rules

grappling: tugging

hydrated: having enough water in the body to keep it functioning correctly

ippon: a score of ten points earned by pinning an opponent to the mat for 30 seconds or throwing an opponent to the mat forcefully

jujitsu: a martial art in which players hit each other with their hands, feet, and elbows

pins: holds down on the mat

spar: train with a partner in judo fighting techniques

tori: the offensive judoka who does the throwing and pinning

uke: the defensive judoka who is thrown or pinned

Index

belt 6, 7, 16
breakfalls 12
danger area 9, 11
diet 20
dojo 6, 8, 10, 22
Douillet, David 19
gi 7, 16
ground holds 12, 15
ippon 5, 10, 15

jujitsu 4, 23
Kano, Jigoro 4, 22, 23
Matsumoto, Sayaka 15, 19
medal 4, 15, 17, 18, 19, 23
Olympic Games 4, 5, 8, 17, 18, 19, 23
Pedro, Jimmy 5, 18, 19
pin 5, 10, 11, 15
sensei 6, 22

stretching 21
Tamura, Ryoko 18
throw 5, 6, 8, 10, 11, 12, 13, 14, 15
tori 10, 12, 13, 15
uke 10, 11, 12, 13, 14, 15
White House 22
World Championships 15, 17, 18, 19

Web Sites

www.JudoInfo.com

www.usjf.com

www.ipl.org/ref/olympics/judo.html

members.nbci.com/jimmypedro/home.html

sports.yahoo.com/oly/judo

www.judocoach.com